Romans, Saxons & Vikings

KT-104-408

Beliefs and Myths of Viking Britain

Martyn Whittock

First published in Great Britain by
Heinemann Library,
Halley Court, Jordan Hill, Oxford OX2 8EJ
a division of Reed Educational & Professional Publishing Ltd.

OXFORD   FLORENCE   PRAGUE   MADRID
ATHENS   MELBOURNE   AUCKLAND
KUALA LUMPUR   SINGAPORE   TOKYO
IBADAN   NAIROBI   KAMPALA
JOHANNESBURG   GABORONE
PORTSMOUTH NH (USA) CHICAGO
MEXICO CITY   SAO PAULO

Designed by Ken Vail Graphic Design

Produced by Celia Floyd

Illustrations by Jeff Edwards

Originated by Magnet Harlequin Group

Printed in Great Britain by
Bath Press Colourbooks, Glasgow

01 00 99 98 97

10 9 8 7 6 5 4 3 2 1

ISBN 0 431 05978 0

British Library Cataloguing in Publication Data

Whittock, Martyn J. (Martyn John)
Beliefs and myths of Viking Britain
1.Vikings – Mythology – Juvenile literature
2.Mythology, British – Juvenile literature
3.Legends – Great Britain – Juvenile literature
I.Title II.Viking Britain
398'.0941

Every effort has been made to contact copyright
holders of any material reproduced in this book.
Any omissions will be rectified in subsequent
printings if notice is given to the Publisher.

For Rosie and Daniel Williams.

Acknowledgements

The Publishers would like to thank the
following for permission to reproduce
photographs.

Ashmolean Museum, Oxford: p. 19 ○
Trustees of the British Library: p. 23 ○
Trustees of the British Museum:
pp. 17, 21 ○ Robert Estall Photographs:
p. 25 ○ Werner Forman Archive: pp. 5,
6, 7, 9, 11, 13, 29 ○ Humberside
Archaeology Unit/Roger Simpson:
p. 15 ○ National Museum of Denmark:
p. 4 ○ National Monuments Record,
Swindon: p. 28 ○ Past Forward, York/
K. S. Gordon: pp. 5, 27

Cover shows Sigurd slaying the Dragon,
carved on the door of Hylestad church
in Norway. Photo courtesy of C. M.
Dixon.

Our thanks to Keith Stringer of the
Department of History of Lancaster
University, for his comments in the
preparation of this book.

We would like to thank the following
Wiltshire schools for valuable
comments made regarding the content
and layout of this series: Fitzmaurice
Primary School, Bradford-on-Avon;
Dauntsey's Primary School, West
Lavington; and Studley Green Primary
School, Trowbridge.

Details of written sources

R.I. Page, *Chronicles of the Vikings*,
British Museum Press 1995: pp. 4A, 8B,
12ABC, 15C, 16AB, 20A ○ D.M. Wilson,
The Northern World, Thames and
Hudson 1980: pp. 6B, 7CD, 8A○
M. Magnuson, *Vikings*, Bodley
Head/BBC 1980: p. 10B ○ J. Simpson,
The Viking World, Batsford 1980: pp.
14AB, 26B ○ G. Garmonsway (trans),
The Anglo Saxon Chronicle, Dent 1972:
p. 17D, 19D, 22A ○ J. Nichol, *The
Vikings*, Blackwell 1979: pp. 18A, 23B ○
L. M. Smith (Ed.), *The making of Britain*,
Macmillan 1984: p. 18B ○ J. Graham-
Campbell, *Cultural Atlas of the Viking
World*, Andromeda 1994: p. 20B, 26A ○
J. Richards, *Viking Age England*,
Batsford/English Heritage 1991:
pp. 21D, 24B, 28A ○ D. J. V. Fisher,
The Anglo-Saxon Age c.400–1042,
Longman 1972: p. 23C

Contents

Clues about Viking beliefs   **4**

The chief pagan gods   **6**

The families of the gods   **8**

Great heroes and legendary creatures   **10**

The end of the world   **12**

Holy places and sacrifices   **14**

Spells and magic   **16**

Vikings and Christians   **18**

Christianity and pagan beliefs   **20**

The triumph of Christianity   **22**

Churches in the Viking age   **24**

Places of the dead   **26**

Changing ideas about death   **28**

Glossary   **30**

Timeline   **31**

Index   **32**

Clues about Viking beliefs

The first Vikings to come to Britain, after AD789, were not Christians. They believed in many gods and goddesses instead of one God. Christians called people like this pagans.

The Vikings who wrote about their **pagan** beliefs did not live in this country. The writers lived in places like Iceland. We do not always know if Vikings believed the same things in Britain. These books were often written hundreds of years after the Viking invasions of Britain. They might have got facts wrong.

Some **Anglo-Saxons** wrote about Viking beliefs but often did not like the Vikings. They may have made them sound bad because of this. Most Vikings became Christian in Britain within a hundred years of first arriving. There is not a lot of evidence here about their pagan beliefs.

Source A

The sun goes dark. The earth sinks into the sea. The bright stars fall from the skies.

A Viking idea about the end of the world. But it was written in Iceland in about AD1000. We do not know if all British Vikings believed this.

Source B

*A box made to keep holy Christian things in. Perhaps it held the bones of a **saint**. It was made in about AD750, in Britain. It was found in Norway. Was it stolen from the Christians? Or was the owner a Viking Christian keeping it safe? We cannot be sure.*

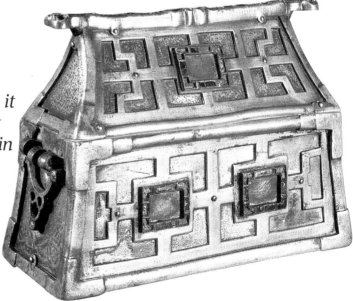

Source C

A mould to make jewellery with. It was made to make Christian crosses and hammer shapes. Hammers were the badge of the pagan god Thor. Vikings may have mixed up religious beliefs. This can make it hard to know what was important to them. This mould was found in Denmark. It is from the tenth century AD.

Source D

Pagan Viking grave, tenth century AD, from Orkney, Scotland. Few pagan Viking graves have been found in Britain. Vikings took on Christian beliefs soon after they settled here. This makes it hard to find out about Viking pagan ideas.

5

The chief pagan gods

The chief pagan Viking gods were Odin and Thor. They were similar to Woden and Thunor, worshipped by pagan Anglo-Saxons.

Odin, god of war

The Viking god of war was named Odin. Most Vikings thought he was the chief god. He had a special horse which had eight legs. This horse was named Sleipnir. Odin lived in a palace called Valhalla. Dead warriors were brought there to serve him. Vikings thought Odin sometimes let his followers die in battle. This made it hard to trust him. The **Anglo-Saxon** name for Odin was Woden. Wednesday was named after him. It means Woden's day, or Odin's day.

Odin the one-eyed god of poetry

Odin was also the god of poetry and magic. He had given one of his eyes to pay for his secret knowledge.

Thor, god of thunder

Thor was god of thunder and lightning. To some Vikings he was the chief god.

A carving of the god Thor. He is fishing for the great snake. He is using an ox head as bait. This is from Gosforth, Cumbria.

Thor glared at the snake. The snake glared back. It blew poison.

Snorri Sturluson wrote this in the thirteenth century AD, in Iceland.

Thor was similar to the Anglo-Saxon **pagan** god Thunor. He was very strong. He had a great hammer named Miollnir. It was made by dwarfs. He fought giants, who were the enemies of the gods.

Sea monsters

The Vikings called the Earth where people lived Midgard. All around was a deep sea, full of monsters. One of these was a great snake called Midgardsorm.

How do we know?

Source B shows that Icelanders thought Thor fought a terrible snake. Source A shows that Viking people in Britain believed the same thing. Source D shows some Vikings thought Thor was the chief god.

Source C shows Odin was thought to have a special horse. We cannot be completely sure that Vikings in Britain believed this, though we know they did in Sweden.

A carving of Odin riding his eight-legged horse, Sleipnir. This was made in about AD850. It is from Gotland, Sweden.

Source D

Jupiter is the chief of all the gods that the **heathen worship**. He is called Thor by some people. The Danish people love him the most.

Written by Elfric, an Anglo-Saxon, in the eleventh century AD. Jupiter was the chief Roman god.

The families of the gods

The Vikings believed in many different gods and goddesses. They believed that they came from two great families.

The Asir

Most gods and goddesses belonged to the family called the Asir. Their home was in a fortress called Asgard. They included Odin and Thor. Sif was Thor's wife. Frigg was the wife of Odin. Their child was Baldr, who was later killed by the wicked god Loki. Tyr was god of warriors.

The Vanir

The other family of gods and goddesses were called the Vanir. They were not as violent as the Asir, who were warrior gods.

The chief Vanir god was Niord, god of the sea. His son was Freyr. His daughter was Freyia. They were god and goddess of love, and were in charge of sunshine and rain.

The world of the gods

Vikings thought Asgard was joined to the earth by a bridge. The bridge was called Bifrost. It looked like a rainbow. They called the Earth Midgard.

Source C

A picture from a church in Sweden. It was made in the twelfth century AD. The large figures are Odin, Thor and Freyr. The little figure is Freyia.

How do we know?

Source A shows that British Vikings **worshipped** the goddess Frigg. They named Friday after her. However, we do not know if they worshipped many of the other gods, apart from Odin and Thor.

Source B shows there were two groups of gods. At first they fought each other.

Source C shows that these different gods later lived together in peace. In this picture there is no fighting between them.

Battles between the gods

At first the Vanir and the Asir fought each other. This was the first war in the world. But in the end they made peace and lived together. Later humans were made to live in the world.

The greatest enemies of the gods were the giants. They wanted to destroy Asgard and kill all the gods.

Great heroes and legendary creatures

The Vikings believed in great heroes. Stories about gods or imaginary people and creatures are called myths, or legends.

Sigurd the dragon killer

Sigurd was a great hero. Viking **myths** say he killed a dragon called Fafnir. Sigurd had a magical sword. He could understand the birds. He captured great amounts of treasure. But in the end he was betrayed and murdered.

The Valkyries

These were mythical women who chose which warriors would die in battle. This was the best way for a warrior to die.

Their name means choosers of the dead. They brought the dead people to Odin.

Elves

In thirteenth century Iceland, Snorri Sturluson wrote that Vikings believed in light elves and dark elves. Dark elves made people sick and caused trouble. Light elves were friendly.

Source A

Prepare the benches,
wash the goblets,
serve the wine.

A Viking poem called Eiriksmal tells how Odin ordered the Valkyries to welcome the dead King Eric Bloodaxe. It was written in the tenth century AD. Eric Bloodaxe was the Viking king of York. He died in northern England in AD954.

Source B

It is terrible now to look around, as a blood-red cloud darkens the sky. The sky is stained with the blood of men as the Valkyries sing their song.

A Viking poem called Darratharljoth. It was written after the battle of Clontarf. This was fought in Ireland in AD1014.

A wooden carving from the story of Sigurd. It shows his sword being made by a man named Regin. This was carved in Norway, in the thirteenth century AD.

How do we know?

Sources A and B show Vikings believed in Valkyries. Source B tells how they visited battlefields. Source A shows they were thought to serve dead warriors in Odin's hall. Both these sources are linked to battles fought in Britain.

Source C shows that Sigurd had a special sword made for him. Source D shows people in Britain knew the story.

Source D

The same story as Source C, on a cross at Halton in Lancashire. Regin is making the sword. It is from the tenth century AD. This is a drawing of it.

The end of the world

A famous Viking myth, or legend, told how the world would finally come to an end.

A legendary creature was the terrible wolf Fenrir. The gods had captured it and chained it up. It was so fierce it had bitten off the hand of the god Tyr. On the last day of the world it would escape. It would invade the world.

The wolf would lead an army to attack Asgard. With it would be giants and the great snake (Midgardsorm) that Thor had once tried to catch. A mighty battle, called Ragnarok, would be fought. The gods would be defeated.

When the gods had finally been beaten, a giant called Surt would destroy the world with fire. But some gods would survive to create a new world which would be all good.

Source A

The wolf Fenrir will gulp down the Father of Men. Vidar will avenge him. He will rip apart its cold jaws, in battle with the wolf.

From a tenth century Viking poem, called Vafthrudnismal. Father of Men is a name for Odin.

Source B

His chains will snap, the wolf runs free.
An axe-age, a sword-age, shields broken.
A wind-age, a wolf-age.
No man will spare his neighbour.

From a poem called Voluspa. It was written in Iceland in about AD1000.

Source C

The wolf will gulp down Odin. That is the end of him. Then Surt will sling fire over the earth and burn the whole world up.

Written by Snorri Sturluson in Iceland, in the thirteenth century AD.

Source D

A carving from a Christian cross. It comes from Kirk Andreas on the Isle of Man. On one side this cross has a picture of Christ defeating evil. On the other side it has this picture of the battle of Ragnarok. The cross was carved in the tenth century AD.

How do we know?

Source A shows Vikings believed the wolf Fenrir would kill Odin. Odin is called Father of Men. This source shows that the wolf would then be killed by another god.

Source B shows this was thought to happen after the wolf had broken its chains. This would lead to a terrible war that would destroy the world.

Source C shows that it was thought a fire giant, called Surt, would then burn up the world.

Viking people in Britain also believed in the great battle of Ragnarok. Source D shows this. It shows Odin being eaten by the wolf.

We can tell it is Odin because he has only one eye. He is shown with a raven. Vikings thought that ravens told Odin what was happening in the world. He had two ravens called Thought and Memory.

Holy places and sacrifices

Pagan Vikings built temples and had special places where they worshipped their gods. Here they often made sacrifices to please them.

Temples

Vikings built special buildings where they **worshipped** their gods. We know about some they built in Iceland, Sweden and Norway.

They were described by Christian writers, many years later. These **temples** contained **altars** and statues of gods, called **idols**. **Sacrifices** were made there.

Archaeologists have never found any of these temples anywhere. Perhaps there were not many of them.

Trees, rivers and springs

Most Viking holy places were probably in the open air. They were not great buildings. Instead, they worshipped at sacred trees, rivers and springs. In Ireland, there was a group of oak trees near Dublin called 'Thor's Grove'.

Source A

A tall, upright wooden post with a face like a man's.

The Arab writer Ibn Fadlan described Viking pagan idols in Russia, in the tenth century AD. Vikings travelled great distances.

Source B

The wizard takes the human, or animal. He ties a rope round its neck. He hangs it from a pole until it dies. He says 'This is an offering to god'.

The Arab Ibn Rustah, wrote this about Vikings in Russia in the tenth century AD.

Near this temple is a huge tree. There is also a well there, where they hold pagan sacrifices. A living man is plunged into it.

Adam of Bremen describing a Viking temple at Uppsala, Sweden. Adam wrote in about AD1070.

Source D

Sacrificed animals found at Skerne, in Yorkshire.

Pagan sacrifices in England

In England there are places where Viking people sacrificed animals to please their gods. At Skerne, in Yorkshire, tenth century Vikings sacrificed dogs, horses and cattle in the River Hull. They also threw a spoon and sword into the water.

About AD1000 Wulfstan, Archbishop of York, said it was wrong to make sacrifices to idols. He said it was wrong to worship **pagan** gods at wells, springs, rocks and trees.

At a Viking **cemetery** on the Isle of Man a woman may have been sacrificed to go with her master to the world of the dead.

How do we know?

Source A shows Vikings worshipped statues. But none have been found in Britain. Sources B and C show that sacrifices were made to the gods. Source D shows that Vikings seem to have done this in Britain. At Skerne, animals were killed. These were probably sacrifices.

15

Spells and magic

The Vikings believed in magic spells. They believed that saying special words could make things happen. These things might be good, or bad.

Runes

These were letters used for writing. Vikings believed Odin knew the secret meanings of **runes**. He had gone through a painful test to earn this knowledge.

Magic spells

Many people thought runes had magic power and could be used to make **magic** spells. They thought these could bring a dead person back to life, or free a person from chains.

But many runes were used for writing, not for magic. They were carved on ordinary things.

Special rings

Vikings believed that some metal rings were holy. If they held one when they made a promise they had to keep the promise. If they broke the promise, something bad would be sure to happen to them.

16

Source C

A comb case from Lincoln. It was made in the tenth or eleventh century AD. Runes on it say: 'Thorfastr made a fine comb'.

Source D

They swore him oaths on the sacred ring. Before this they would never swear these oaths to outsiders.

From the Anglo-Saxon Chronicle, AD875. An oath is a very serious promise. The promise described here was made by Vikings to Alfred, king of Wessex.

How do we know?

Source A shows Viking people believed the pagan god Odin knew the meaning of runes. He had paid for the knowledge by suffering pain. At the end of this painful test he understood the runes' secrets. But Source C shows that runes could be used for very ordinary messages.

Source B shows that Vikings believed magic spells could make things happen. Source D shows that special rings were used for swearing oaths. Vikings thought it wrong to break an oath sworn while holding one of these rings.

Viking (Danish) runes

f   u   th o r k h n i a s t b m l

Vikings and Christians

The first Vikings in Britain attacked and robbed Christian holy places. Later they began to respect Christian ideas.

The first Vikings, in the eighth and ninth centuries, attacked Christian churches. They stole things from them made of gold and silver. Sometimes they killed the people that they caught there. These attacks shocked and frightened people.

It looked as if the Vikings hated Christians. But this is probably not true. They attacked the churches because there was treasure there. There was no-one to defend it. The Vikings were not out to kill Christians. They were out to steal treasure.

Vikings become Christians

Some Viking leaders became Christians in Britain. One, named Guthrum, was persuaded to become a Christian. This was because he was defeated by the Christian **Anglo-Saxon** King Alfred in AD878. We do not know if Guthrum really believed in Jesus. We cannot tell what he thought. But he did stop attacking Wessex.

Source A

They trampled the holy places with foul footsteps. They dug up **altars**. They seized all the treasures of the holy church.

*Simeon of Durham wrote this in about AD1100. He is describing the Viking attack on the **monastery** at Lindisfarne. This happened in AD793.*

Source B

Saint Edmund's ribs were laid bare by numberless gashes. It was as if he had been tortured, or torn apart by savage claws.

This describes how Vikings killed King Edmund of East Anglia. He was later made a saint. This was written in the late tenth century AD, in what is now France.

A Viking silver penny. It was made in about AD890. It has the name of Saint Edmund on it.

The Viking army gave him hostages and solemn oaths that they would leave his kingdom. And they promised that, as well as this, their king would be **baptised**.

The Anglo-Saxon Chronicle, AD878. It describes how the defeated Viking King Guthrum promised King Alfred of Wessex that he would become a Christian.

Edmund – king and saint

In AD869 King Edmund of East Anglia was killed by Viking raiders. He was a Christian. Before long, Anglo-Saxons began to say Edmund had been a saint. This word means a specially holy person. They called him this because he had been killed in a terrible way by **pagans**.

Soon, though, Vikings were treating him like a saint too! By AD890 they were making coins which had his name on them. They went on making these coins into the early tenth century AD. By this time the Vikings had captured large parts of Christian Anglo-Saxon England. They had taken over the beliefs of the people who lived there. Less than 100 years after the first Viking invaders had attacked Christian churches, their children's children had become Christians themselves.

How do we know?

Source A shows that Vikings destroyed Christian holy places. But this does not mean they hated Christians. Source B shows how Vikings killed King Edmund. Source C shows that they were soon treating him as a saint though.

Christianity and pagan beliefs

Vikings encouraged a revival of pagan beliefs in Anglo-Saxon England.

Before the Vikings came some **Anglo-Saxons** had old **pagan** beliefs, but most Anglo-Saxons were Christians. Some pagan beliefs in Britain may have survived from Roman times. The arrival of pagan Vikings may have encouraged these people. Christians in Britain worked hard to stop these ideas from spreading.

Mixing different beliefs

The first Vikings often mixed Christian and pagan beliefs. In York, Christian and pagan pictures were both put on the same coins. In York and on the Isle of Man this happened with carvings too.

Pagan beliefs in England

A lot of Viking swords, axes, tools and other objects have been found in English rivers. They were probably **sacrifices** made to pagan gods. Christians thought this was very wrong.

Laws to stop pagan beliefs

By about AD1000 many Vikings in northern England had become

Source A

He believed in Christ. But he prayed to Thor before sea journeys and when the going got tough.

A Viking story tells how a man called Helgi the Skinny mixed up his beliefs. He came from the Hebrides. These are islands west of Scotland.

Source B

No trying to speak with dead people.
No trying to tell the future.
No using **magic** spells.
No singing pagan songs.
No worshipping pagan gods.
No worshipping the sun, moon, fire, water.

Rules made by Wulfstan, Archbishop of York, AD1002.

Source C

It is against the law to worship **idols**, heathen gods, the sun or moon, fire or flood, springs, stones, or any kind of tree.

Laws of King Cnut; made around AD1020.

Christians. But some kept on **worshipping** pagan gods.

Archbishop Wulfstan lived in York. He spoke out against pagan beliefs and said they were wrong. People did what he said. In about AD1020 King Cnut made Wulfstan's ideas into laws. These punished people for worshipping pagan gods.

How do we know?

Source A shows that some Vikings mixed up pagan and Christian beliefs.

Source D shows that Vikings in England probably sacrificed objects in rivers. Source B shows that Anglo-Saxon Christians wanted to stop things like this. Source C shows that kings made laws to stop pagan beliefs.

Source D

A stirrup from the tenth century AD. It was found in the river Witham, Lincolnshire. Quite a few precious objects like this have been found in rivers and were probably sacrifices.

The triumph of Christianity

The Vikings who settled in Britain became Christians. This was helped by their Viking kings becoming Christians.

Some **Anglo-Saxon** rulers wanted Viking leaders to become Christians. They hoped this would stop them attacking England.

Olaf Tryggvason joins the Christians

In AD994 the Anglo-Saxon King Ethelred persuaded a Viking leader who had already been baptised to stop attacking Christians. This Viking leader was Olaf Tryggvason. Olaf then forced other Vikings to become Christians, and he himself stopped attacking Anglo-Saxon England.

King Cnut – Christian Viking king

The Viking leader, Cnut, (sometimes spelt 'Canute') conquered England in AD1016. He became king of England, Denmark and Norway. At a meeting held at Oxford, in AD1018, he promised to defend Christianity. Between AD1020 and 1023 he passed laws protecting the Christian religion.

Source A

The king sent Bishop Elfhere to fetch Olaf. King Ethelred stood sponsor for him before the bishop. Olaf said he would not attack England again. He kept his promise.

*The Anglo-Saxon Chronicle, AD994. The words 'stood sponsor' means that Olaf was **confirmed** as a Christian.*

Source B

Olaf spoke to him in this way. 'It is my will that you will be baptised and all your followers. Otherwise, you will be killed right here.' Then all the Orkneys became Christian.

The Orkneyinga Saga tells how Olaf forced the pagan Viking ruler of the Orkney islands to become a Christian.

Source C

They would always only honour one God and firmly believe in one Christian faith.

Promises made by Cnut and his supporters at Oxford in AD1018.

Source D

A picture drawn in about AD1020. It shows Cnut and his wife giving a cross to a church at Winchester.

The triumph of Christianity

Viking **pagan** beliefs changed to Christian ones. This was helped by Viking leaders becoming Christians. These leaders punished people who kept **worshipping** the pagan gods. They helped pagans think it was right to become Christian.

Cnut sent Anglo-Saxon Christians to preach to pagans living in Denmark. Viking kings of Norway asked Anglo-Saxons to help them spread Christian beliefs. They went to preach in Norway and Sweden.

How do we know?

Source A shows that Anglo-Saxon kings were keen for Viking rulers to become Christians. When Olaf was confirmed, he stopped attacking England. Source B shows he made other Vikings become Christians too.

Sources C and D show that the Viking Cnut supported Christianity. He promised to live as a Christian. He gave presents to churches.

Churches in the Viking age

In areas the Vikings captured, after about AD850, Christian Anglo-Saxons carried on using their churches. Soon Viking Christians began to build churches too.

Churches from the Viking age

Many Vikings soon became Christians. New churches were built in the areas they ruled. Some were built of wood and were not very large. Churches like this were built at North Elmham in Norfolk and at Stafford in Staffordshire. Later stone churches were built in these places. Other churches were larger buildings. The fact that wars were being fought between **Anglo-Saxons** and Vikings did not stop them from being built.

Source A

Orm, son of Gamal, bought St Gregory's church when it was ruined and tumbled down. He had it completely rebuilt in honour of Christ.

A carving on the wall of Kirkdale church, in Yorkshire. Orm and Gamal are Viking names. The words were carved in about AD1055.

Source B

Plan of the church built in the Viking age at North Elmham, Norfolk.

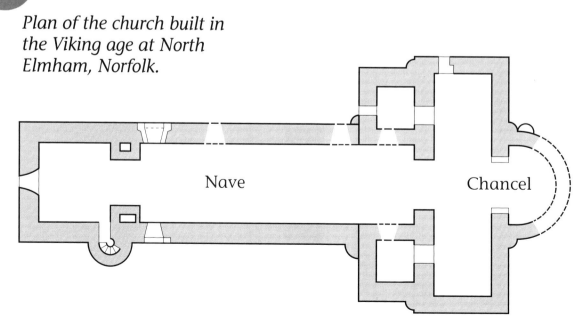

Nave

Chancel

The wooden stave church at Greensted, Essex.

How do we know?

Source A shows that Viking Lords built churches. Source C shows a church built in a Viking way. Most were not built like this. Most churches in Viking areas were the same as churches in Anglo-Saxon areas.

Viking style churches?

It is hard to find churches from the Viking age. Many were altered in later years. **Archaeologists** have to look at buildings very carefully. They look for clues in the way they were built. They look for different kinds of decoration. Churches built in Viking areas of England were no different from ones built in areas they did not rule. They must have used Anglo-Saxon builders and ideas, instead of bringing in new ideas of their own. The only differences were in the way some crosses and gravestones were decorated.

Most churches were built with a small place for the priest to lead **worship** (the chancel). The people stood in a larger part called the nave. There was often a tower at the western end. Many fine towers were built in Viking areas of Lincolnshire, East Anglia and Northumbria.

There is just one church which seems different. It is in Greensted, Essex, and has survived from Viking times. It is called a 'stave' church – which means its walls are made from planks of wood. Churches like this were built in Norway, Denmark and Sweden.

Places of the dead

Pagan Vikings buried their dead differently from Christians. Very few of these pagan burials have been found in Britain.

Grave-goods and burial mounds

Pagan Vikings buried people with their belongings. **Archaeologists** call these belongings grave-goods. Vikings thought the dead people could use these things in the world of the dead. The graves of rich people were sometimes covered with mounds of earth. Vikings sometimes burnt the bodies of dead people. This is called **cremation**.

Pagan burials in England

Very few pagan Viking graves have been found in England. This probably shows that Vikings soon copied Christian ways of burying dead people. Anglo-Saxon Christians did not cremate people, or bury them with grave-goods.

Only about thirty pagan Viking burial places have been found in England. The bodies in many of these graves were not cremated. But some cremated Vikings were buried at Ingleby, in Derbyshire. Here sixty burial mounds were put up over the ashes of the dead.

Source A

Odin made a law. All dead men should be burnt. And their belongings should be put with them on the fire. Their ashes should be thrown into the sea, or buried in the ground.

The Icelander Snorri Sturluson wrote this in the thirteenth century AD.

Source B

When a great man dies, they make a grave like a house. They put him in it. With him they put his clothes, gold arm-rings and also much food. They also put his wife in the grave with him, while she is still alive.

Written by an Arab, Ibn Rustah. He met Vikings in Russia, in the tenth century AD.

Source C

A Viking buried under a boat, on the Orkney islands. The boat has rotted. Its shape can be seen.

Viking Pagan burials in England.

Pagan Viking graves in Scotland and on the Isle of Man

Some pagan Viking graves have been found in Scotland. On the Orkney islands two men were buried with boats over them. A few pagan graves have been found on the Hebrides islands, but only a few.

On the Isle of Man many pagan burials have been found. Some people were buried under boats. In three graves it seems that women were killed to be buried with men. These women may have been slaves, or wives.

How do we know?

Source A shows some Vikings cremated dead people. They also burnt their grave goods. Some thought Odin had said they should do this. But Source B shows that not all Vikings cremated their dead. Source C shows this too. Source B also shows that sometimes women were forced to be buried with rich Viking men. This happened on the Isle of Man too.

Changing ideas about death

Vikings in Britain soon began to copy
Christian ways of burying people.

Pagan burials at churches

Some **pagan** burials, from
the tenth century AD, have
been found in, or near,
Christian churches. These Vikings
buried their dead in Christian
cemeteries. But they buried
them in a pagan way. They
buried them with their
belongings. Burials like these
have been found under Carlisle
Cathedral, in Cumbria. At
Kildale, in Yorkshire, Vikings
were buried under the church.
One was buried with an axe.
Three more were buried with
their swords.

Some of these Vikings may have
been Christians, but they still
buried their dead in the old
pagan way. Or they may have
been pagans. They might have
just used the Christian churches
and cemeteries because they were
holy places. They might have
done it to show they had taken
over Christian places. At
Balladoole, on the Isle of Man,
Vikings buried two people in a
boat. They did it in a Christian
cemetery. But they destroyed the
Christian graves already there.

Source A

Gurnkel set up this stone
in memory of Gunnar,
his father. Helgi buried
him in a stone coffin,
in England at Bath.

*From a carved stone
found at Navelsjo,
in Sweden.*

Source B

*A carved grave-stone.
It was found at St Paul's
Cathedral, London.*
Runes *on it say: 'Ginna
and Toki had this stone
put up'. The carving
on it is a kind used
by Vikings.*

Source C

Stones covering graves. These were found under York Minster. They have carvings on them in the Viking style. They probably date from the tenth century AD.

Christian Viking burials

Most Vikings buried their dead in the Christian way. It is hard to tell if these graves are graves of Vikings. This is because they were not buried with Viking objects.

There are some clues though. Sometimes special stones were put over the graves. These were decorated with Viking patterns. There are some under York Minster. In other places strangely carved stones were put up, called Hogbacks. But they may just have belonged to **Anglo-Saxons** who liked Viking fashions.

Most Vikings copied Christian ways of burial. Some used stone coffins. Some used wooden ones. Most buried people in simple holes.

Glossary

Anglo-Saxons people living in England when the Vikings invaded

altar a stone on which sacrifices were made to Viking gods; the stone table in a Christian church where the priest said mass

archaeologists people who dig up and study things made in the past

baptise people are baptised with water, as a sign they are joining the Christian church

cemetery a place where the dead are buried

confirmation when a person renews their promises to believe in Christianity and live as a Christian. It happens after baptism.

cremation burning dead bodies

heathen followers of a non-Christian religion

idol statue of a pagan god or goddess

magic words, or actions, thought to make things happen by a mysterious power

monastery place where monks and nuns live

myth a story about the gods, or imaginary people to explain things about the world. Also called a **legend**.

pagans followers of a non-Christian religion

runes a type of Viking and Anglo-Saxon writing. The two different peoples used different kinds of runes.

sacrifice giving something to the pagan gods, often an animal's life

saints people who lived holy lives and were prayed to after they had died

temple a place where Viking pagan gods were worshipped

worship praising and showing respect to God or the gods

Timeline – Romans, Anglo-Saxons and Vikings

Viking Age

AD1
AD100
AD200
AD300
AD400
AD500
AD600
AD700
AD800
AD900
AD1000
AD1100

AD700

AD793	Vikings attack Lindisfarne monastery
AD800	
AD869	King Edmund of East Anglia killed by Vikings
AD875	Vikings swear oath to King Alfred on a holy ring. They promise to leave Wessex.
AD878	Guthrum baptised as a Christian
AD890	Vikings treat dead King Edmund of East Anglia as a saint
AD900	
AD954	Death of King Eric Bloodaxe, last pagan Viking king of York
AD994	Olaf Tryggvason confirmed
AD995	Vikings in the Orkneys become Christians
	Archbishop Wulfstan writes against pagan beliefs
AD1000	
AD1018	King Cnut promises to defend Christianity at a meeting in Oxford
AD1020	King Cnut makes laws against pagan worship
AD1070	Adam of Bremen writes about a pagan Viking temple in Sweden
AD1100	

Index

Numbers in plain type (15) refer to the text. Numbers in italic type (*27*) refer to a caption.

Adam of Bremen . . . 15
Alfred, King. 17, 18
altars. 14, 18
Anglo-Saxon Chronicle
. . . . 17, 19, 22
Anglo-Saxons 4
Asgard 8, 9, 12
Asir 8, 9

baptism. 19, 22
battles 10, 11, 12
burial mounds 26
burials 26–9, *27*

carvings *6, 11, 13,*
. . . . *28, 29, 29*
cemeteries . . . 15, 28, 29
Christians. 4, 18–19, 20,
. . . . . 22–3, 24, 26, 28
churches . . . *9,* 18, 24–5,
. . . . *24, 25,* 28
Cnut, King 21, 22, 23, *23*
coffins 28, 29
coins 19, *19,* 20
comb case *17*
cremation 26, 27

Denmark. 23, 25

Elfric 7, 8
elves 10
end of the world
. . . . 4, 12, 13
Eric Bloodaxe 10
Ethelred, King 22

Fenrir. 12, 13
Freyia 8, *9*
Freyr 8, *9*
Frigg 8, *9*

giants 6, 9, 12, 13

gods and goddesses
. . . . 6–9, 12, 13
grave-goods. 26, 27
grave-stones . *28, 29, 29*
graves 5, 26, 27
Greensted 25, *25*
Guthrum 18, 19

hammers. *5,* 6
Hebrides 20, 27
heroes 10
Hogbacks 29
holy places 14, 15

Ibn Fadlan 14
Ibn Rustah 14, 26
Iceland
. . . . 4, 6, 8, 10, 12, 14
idols. 14, 15
Ingleby 26
Ireland 10, 14
Isle of Man *13,* 15,
. . . . 20, 27, 28

jewellery *5*
Jupiter 7

legends 10, 12
Lindisfarne 18

magic 16, 17
Midgard 8
Midgardsorm 7, 12
monasteries. 18
myths 10, 12

Norway *4, 11,* 14, 23, 25

oaths 17, 19
Odin . . . 6, 7, *7,* 8, *9,* 10,
12, 13, 16, 17, 26, 27
Orkney . . . *5,* 22, 27, *27*

pagans . . . 4, 14, 19, 20,
. . . . . . 21, 23, 26, 28
poems 8, 10, 12, 16

Ragnarok, battle of
. . . . 12, 13, *13*
rings 16, 17
runes . . . 16, 17, *17, 28*
Russia 14, 26

sacrifices. . . . 14, 15, *15,*
. . . . 20, 21, *21*
Saint Edmund
. . . . 18, 19, *19*
saints. 4, 19
sea monsters 7
Sigurd 10, 11, *11*
Simeon of Durham . . 18
Skerne 15, *15*
Sleipnir 6, *7*
spells 16, 17
statues. 14, 15
stirrup *21*
Sturluson, Snorri
. . . . 6, 10, 12, 26
Surt 12, 13
Sweden *9,* 14, 15, 23, 25

temples 14, 15
Thor. . *5, 6, 6, 7,* 8, *9,* 12
treasure. 18
Tryggvason, Olaf 22, 23

Valhalla 6
Valkyries 10, 11
Vanir 8, 9

Woden. 6
Wulfstan, Archbishop
. . . . 15, 20, 21

York. 20, 29, *29*